"Like a good gin and tonic."
Lemn Sissay

"Moving, amusing, revealing and compelling."
Jonathan Ross

"Dan Cockrill is a poet of nuance, whispers and extraordinary beauty, who holds his pen as though it were the pointer on a compass. These poems navigate between worlds and map the distance between them, drawing them together. These are impossible poems, small things which contain the universe. Each poem is a response to a picture, each picture drawn in response to a poem. This is a book of circles. Own it."
Joelle Taylor

"Cor, I love this book, such a lovely turn of phrase and sensitivity and humour. This book is playful and profound, surreal and laugh out loud funny. There is a wonderful comedy and romance in here, a beautiful collaboration and a colourful celebration of the now."
Salena Godden

"Damien Weighill draws pictures that feed words into your head. Daniel Cockrill writes words that feed pictures into your head. By the time I got to the end of this book I had a casserole of life in my head and I'm still eating it now."
Rob Auton

"Dan Cockrill is a very human human and, as both poet and person, he approaches this mad, sad, beautiful world with the perfect combination of playfulness and betrayed disappointment. What I love about his writings is what I love about life: One moment it has you giggling at the daftness of it all; the next it just breaks your heart."
Jonny Fluffypunk

Daniel Cockrill

Daniel Cockrill's words have appeared in books, newspapers, magazines, on gallery walls and have been spoken out loud on stage, radio and television. He is the Co-founder of Bang Said The Gun and Page Match. He lives and works in London.

www.danielcockrill.com

Damien Weighill

Born in the North East of England and now based in London. Damien Weighill creates illustrations full of ideas for a host of international clients. His comic strips have been published regularly in The Sunday Times Magazine.

www.damienweighill.com

In The Beginning Was The Word

**THEN A DRAWING, THEN MORE WORDS,
ANOTHER DRAWING, AND SO ON AND SO ON**

**Daniel Cockrill
Damien Weighill**

Burning Eye

BurningEyeBooks
Never Knowingly Mainstream

Poems copyright © 2017 Daniel Cockrill
Illustrations copyright © 2017 Damien Weighill

The authors assert the moral right under the Copyright, Designs and Patents Act 1988 to be identified as the author of this work.

All rights reserved. No part of this publication may be reproduced, stored in a retrieval system, or transmitted, in any form or by any means without the prior written consent of the author, nor be otherwise circulated in any form of binding or cover other than that in which it is published and without a similar condition being imposed on the subsequent purchaser.

This edition published by Burning Eye Books 2017

www.burningeye.co.uk

@burningeyebooks

Burning Eye Books
15 West Hill, Portishead, BS20 6LG

ISBN 978-1-911550-07-3

For Billy and Finn

CONTENTS

Words
- 11 -

Drawing
- 12 -

Words
- 13 -

Drawing
- 14 -

Some more words
- 15 -

Another drawing
- 16 -

Words again
- 17 -

Then a drawing
- 18 -

More words
- 19 -

A drawing
- 20 -

Words
- 21 -

Another Drawing
- 22 -

More words
- 23 -

Another Drawing
- 24 -

Words again
- 25 -

Drawing
- 26 -

More words
- 27 -

Drawing
- 28 -

Words again
- 29 -

Drawing
- 30 -

Words
- 31 -

Drawing
- 32 -

Words
- 33 -

Double page drawing
- 34 -

Back to the words
- 36 -

Another drawing
- 37 -

Words again
- 38 -

Drawing again
- 39 -

More words
- 40 -

More drawing
- 41 -

Words
- 42 -

Drawing
- 43 -

Words
- 44 -

Drawing
- 45 -

Words and drawing
- 46 -

And more drawing
- 47 -

Back to just words
- 48 -

Some more drawing
- 49 -

A lot of words
- 50 -

Words and drawing
- 51 -

More words
- 52 -

Another drawing
- 53 -

Some more words
- 54 -

A drawing
- 55 -

A few more words
- 56 -

A drawing
- 58 -

Some words
- 59 -

Another drawing
- 60 -

A few more words
- 61 -

A final drawing
- 62 -

And some words to finish
- 63 -

THE UNIVERSE

I wrote one verse
and I called it
The Universe

A ROLLING STONE GATHERS NO COSMOS

whenhetypeditwaslikehewasperformingapianoconcertotounknown
planets//hepunchedthekeyslikemeteorshittingdistantmoons//luna
rockfontscarvingoutcraters//everyletteraBigBangonablankpage//
cometslikequotationmarks//colonslaidoutlikeastronomymaps//
therhythmofSaturn'sribbonspool//thespeedatwhichhescrawled//
acircusofwhirlingstardust
                        spawning
                              asprawling
                                      manyarmed
                                              grandclockwork
planetarium//areamofpaper//abeamoflight//astreamofconsciousness//
butheneverlethismindwanderfar//andheneveronceusedthespacebar//
heneveronceusedthespacebar

MANCRUELMANKINDMANCRAWLMANFINDMANBLIND

In the asteroid evening he dreams of wind farms and discotheques
stares into the unknown
finds he is alone
whispers 'one day son this will all be yours'
with a head full of sawdust and wars
sets ablaze everything we knew
in the fires he grew
scripts containing answers
to our most burning question

Why?

He wants to be the person he used to know
because all the knowledge in the world
is like landing on the moon
it's not really a place you want to stick around

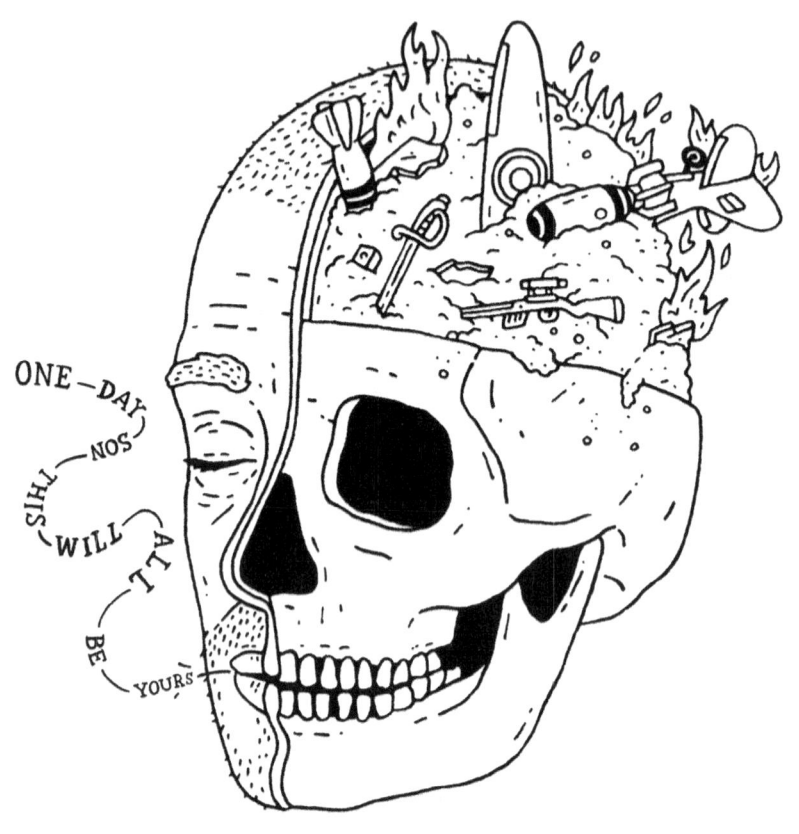

MACHETE HEAD

A head full of swagger
A head full of sewer
A head full of clutter
A head full of scrap metal
A head full of hash
A head full of mustard gas
A head full of chips and peas
A head full of chimpanzees
A head full of killer bees
A head full of memories
A head full of distant planes
cutting through the sky
like death
A head full of blood
A head full of concrete
A head full of dead meat
A head full of Twitter feeds
A head full of nose bleeds
A head full of hateful
of heart full of spiteful
A head full of skin full
A head full of plutonium
A head full of buckets and bullets
of land mines and atom bombs
A head full of ethnic cleansing
A head full of mass graves
A head full of scowl
A head full scars
A head full of crushed cars
A head full of late bars
A head full of dead stars

A head full of static
A head full of rhetoric
A head full of sick
A head full of prick
A head full of smut
A head full of slut
A head full of scum
A head full of cum
A head full of cunt
A head full of can't
A head full of Kant
A head full of fuck
A head full of fascism,
racism, sexism, sarcasm
A head full of chasms
A head full of bad jokes
A head full of rape jokes,
racist jokes, sexist jokes,
homophobic jokes
A head full of fake laughter
A head full of empty laughter
A head full of echoing halls
A head full of stabbings
and sawdust
A head full of fever
A head full of medication
A head full of bent spoons
A head full of broken moons
A head full of warfare
A head full of war fear
It's lonely in here

I'm bent buckled collapsed folded and **MOON RAPED**
With nothing to do except chat shit get pissed sniff glue
hang out in the dark

float in space

A thousand ants drill my skull for oil / A swarm of wasps sting
and pierce my blind Atlantic eyes / A billion parasites blister my
skin with their bombing and blasting and digging and scooping
and gouging and felling and mining and spoiling and poisoning
and polluting / My hair is receding / I wouldn't mind / I'm only
4.5 billion years old

What's the point of all this drunken spinning?

Sunlight finds me curled around the toilet bowl with gag and hurl
plastered to my lips and earthly cheek

U S AY
   Pissed **UP** and retching
On your literature, your art, your underground scene,
your whiskey, your spirit, your sport, your film, your tv,
your theatre, your cartoons and your gun

An avalanche
An overdose of opulence

Teeming in swimming in
Sapped, spent and spat out

Abandoning the brave
Peeled off the earth like a plaster
An unwanted tattoo that reads
'Look at the United State of Us'

BOXED UP

I coulda had class
I coulda been a contender
I coulda been somebody
Instead of a tortoise hibernating in the airing cupboard
Which is what I am
Let's face it

Float like a drug addict
Sting like a urine infection

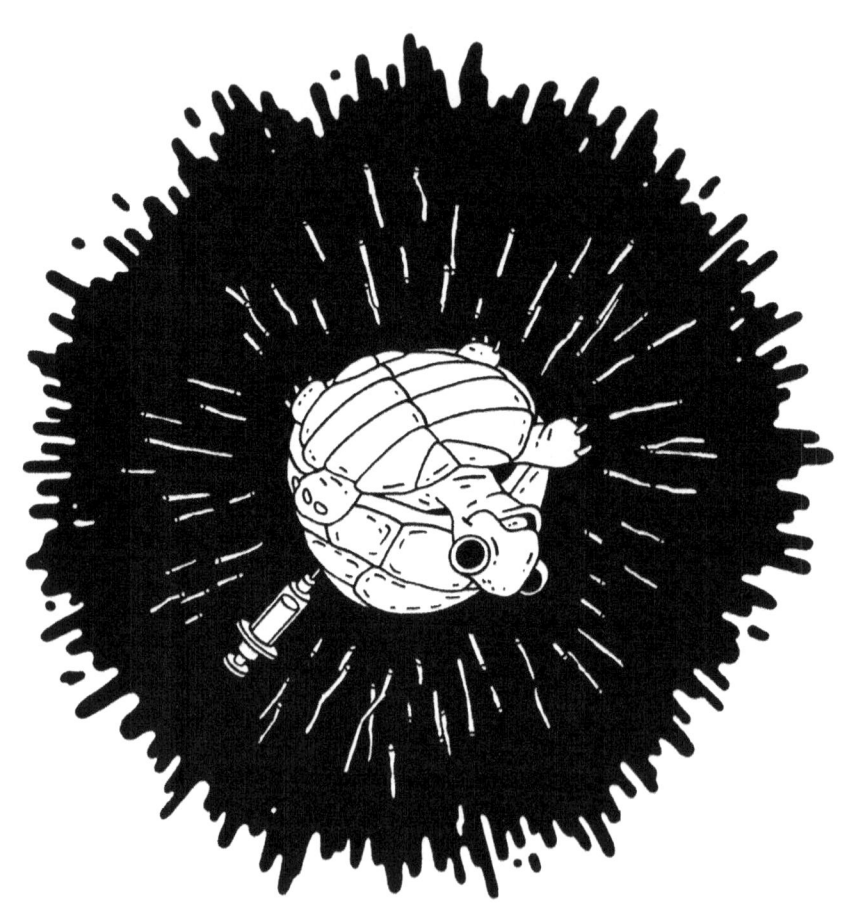

TEENAGE MUTANT BINGER TURTLE

Intergalactic Galapagos land giant
Godless ganja gangster
Shoot up, spin out, smack head, crack whore
It's fucking whizzy

Toke time tortoise
Smoking Don Juan
5, 4, 3, 2… chug on a fat one
Blaze on Purple Haze
Blast a joint
We have lift off

Glide between galaxies
Tumbling turtle hurtling through outer space
A space cadet with wide flying saucer shell eyes
Houston, we have a drug problem
Lettuce pray

Our Father
Cowabunga
CowaBonga
CowaGanja Dude

WHO GOES THERE? FRIEND OR U.F.OE?

I swear I saw God through the swirling haze of octopus tentacles
Hauling me up, heaving me in to some kind of Heaven
Like a slow chug of a steam train approaching a distant station
And on arrival discovering a pub on the platform

QUESTIONS FOR GOD AT BEDTIME

Do you smoke in bed?
If you do are you worried about setting fire to your duvet?
Are your pillows stuffed with cloud or eiderdown?
Is your mattress firm?
Do you sleep in a single or double or kingsize bed?
Is your bed comfortable?
Do you own a teddy bear?
Do you get tucked in at night?
Do you wear pyjamas?
If you eat toast in your cloud bed does it get covered in crumbs?
How often do you change your sheets?
Is there anything that keeps you awake at night?
Things like, "Have I forgotten to lock the front door?"
Do you get up to check or just leave it till the morning only
to discover your television and credit cards have been stolen?
Do you have duvet days?
Do you keep porn under your mattress?
Do you masturbate into a sock to save the sheets?
Do you have wet dreams?
Do you have a recurring dream where you are falling or flying
or your teeth are falling out?
Do you wonder what the dream means?
Do you appear in your own dreams?
Are you a dream?
Are your dreams really nightmares?
Do you struggle to get out of bed in the morning?
Do you wonder what you have created?
Do you think to yourself, "What have I done?"

CLOUDS AND CIGARETTES

Look at the shape of that cloud
It looks like it's smoking a cigarette with its eyes closed
You look up
Your face changes like a cloud changes shape
Like the time you found out your dad used to beat you with a leather belt
And lock you up for hours in a small dark cupboard under the stairs
After remembering this locked away memory
You smoke whole cigarettes in one drag

CIGARETTES AND CLOUDS

Do you remember when all the girls used to smoke cigarettes
In the pubs and the clubs
And when you kissed them in the dark
With your hand up their skirt
Their tongues tasted rough with nicotine?
It was exciting and it was dirty
It made them uglier and more interesting than they could ever imagine
You'd return home alone
Stumbling pissed to your parents' house
Fall rolling and dizzy onto your undersized mattress
Only to wake in the morning heat
With your clothes and room smelling like an ash tray

Nothing was folded neatly
You had knots in your hair
Holes in your shoes
But everything seemed okay
I miss those days

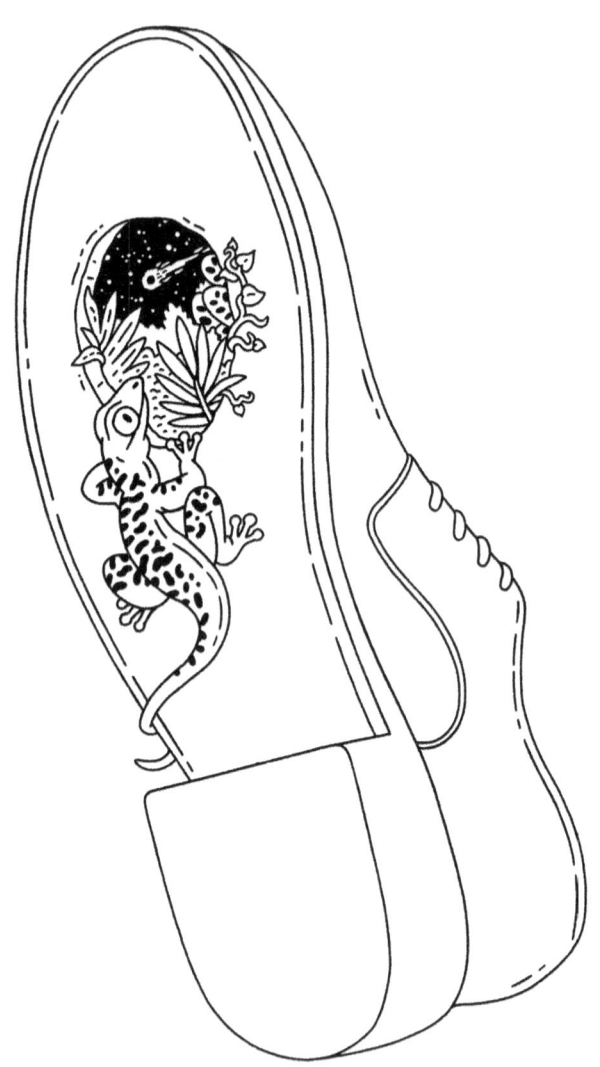

MULTIVERSE

Hope is a shoe with a hole
in its soul, that has walked
many roads, dirt tracks,
cobbled streets, footpaths,
motorway verges, overgrown
cornfields, muddy pools,
stepped through the deepest
puddles and darkest rains,
soaking weary feet for days
or even years

An alternative version of this
poem co-exists on another
page, in another book, on a
different shelf, in a different
room, held open by another
man's hands, with weary feet,
wearing a shoe with a hole
in its soul

THE POEM

Every person who has ever read this poem, or as many like to call it, 'The Poem', have never been able to agree on its actual meaning. Distinguished and acclaimed professors, scholars, scientists, philosophers, political and religious leaders have all spent many hours discussing, analyzing, interpreting and arguing the content and significance of the words in front of them without ever coming up with a comprehensive and conclusive explanation of what the text actually means. What they do agree on though, and as a consequence of their disagreements, is that after reading The Poem many people must die.

Nota bene: The author of 'The Poem' is a pacifist.

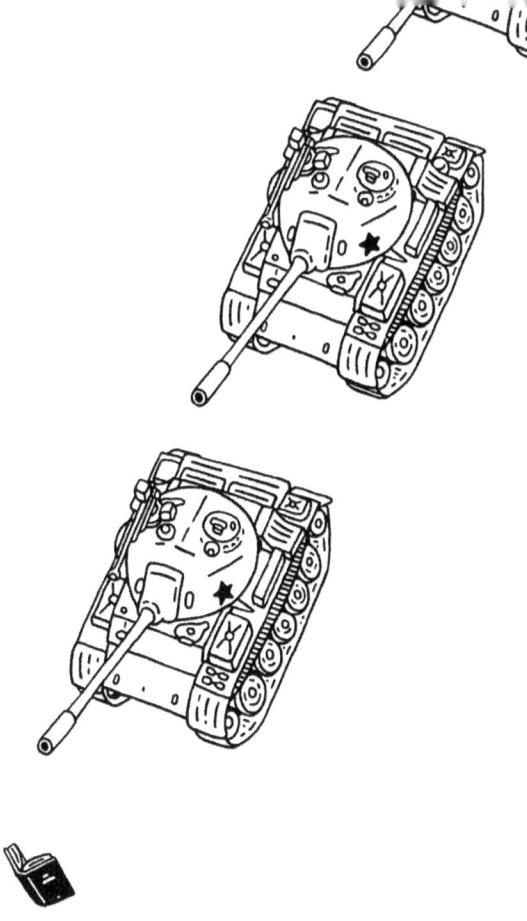

THE BOY WHO DANCED WITH TANKS

You will not pass this way
You will not pass my Paso Doble
Dance with me
With gentle cannon fodder footsteps

A caterpillar Conga
Morris the military men
Foxtrot tank track tyre
Tap to the rhythm of machine gun fire

An ironclad Flamenco
A fighting Fandango
Rumba as they rumble
To the Beijing Bolshevik Bop
Bring the killing machines to a stop

Trapeze the turret
Hold bulletproof metal tightly in my soft silent human arms
Look hard down my gun barrel stare
It's the Last Tango in Tiananmen Square

Do the Cha Cha China
It's Strictly Commie Dancing

The Judges' scores
Vladimir Lenin Goodman
"Seven"

left right left right left right left…

THE GIRL WHO SWAM WITH SUBMARINES

When she was young she dreamed of swimming with dolphins
By the time she was old enough all the dolphins had been maimed and killed
Their carcasses washed up on beaches around the globe

So she organized a movement
Of open water swimmers, surfers and old sea dogs
To circle the warships and submarines
All united in their vision
All swimming in the same direction
All speaking the same language in a thousand different tongues
A Peace On Earth Movement
In short
A P.O.E.M.

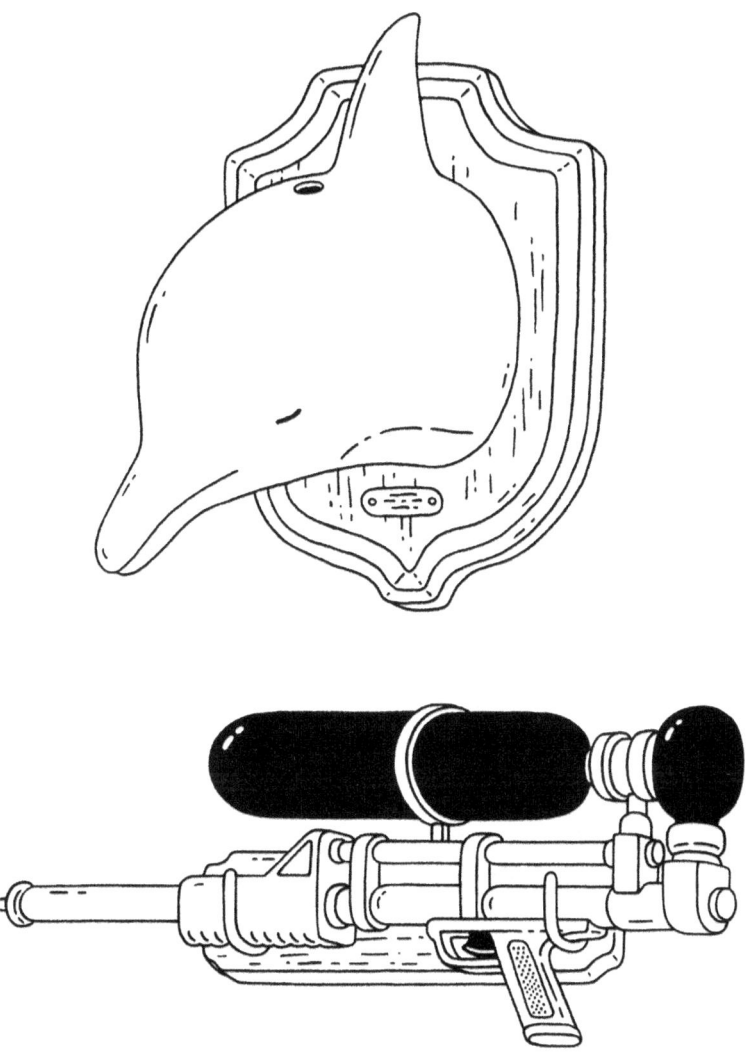

WHAT'S THE PURPOSE OF THE WALL-MOUNTED PORPOISE?

Bang bang bottlenose
Pop shot through the blowhole
Dead Dido dolphin
D'ya mean Dodo?
No
But Dido's not dead though
Oh Dodo
Dead Dodo dolphin
Stupid click click click aquatic grin

Jump through hoops
Flip oversized beach-balls high in the air
Swim in circles
Make a big splash
A big fish in a small pond

What's the purpose of the porpoise?
I don't know
It's pointless

DUCHAMP DOLPHIN

I managed to hole-punch a live bottlenose dolphin
and connect it to the sprinkler system in the garden
Good for the lawn and good for the kids to jump through

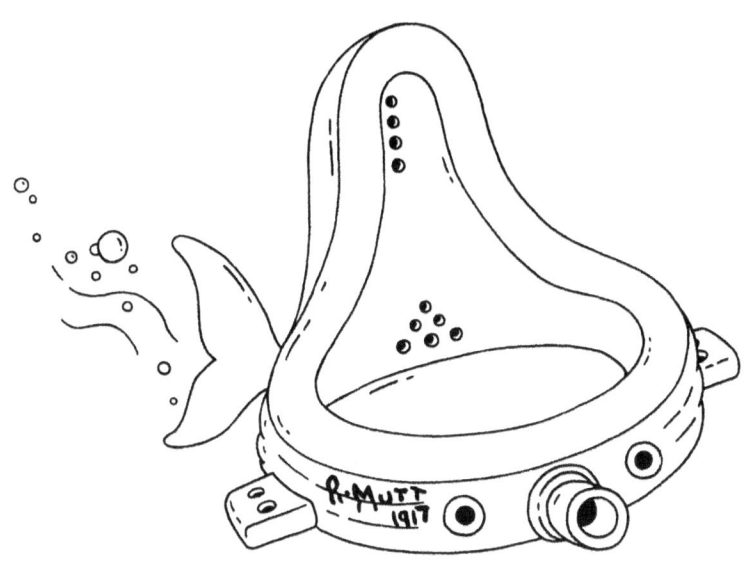

THE PISSER

Some people might not know what goes on at the men's urinal.
Well, it's pretty much eyes down like bingo, face the front, piss.

Don't look left, don't look right, don't judge.

Keep it completely straight. No banter.
Unless you are drunk and in a friendly boozer.

That is the rules
That is the urinal etiquette.

But me
No, not me
I'm like
Grab a cock to the left of me
Grab a cock to the right
And whizz it all around
Make some shapes
You know
Up and down
Round and round
As if holding a sparkler on bonfire night.
Sometimes I spell my name in urine on the porcelain bowl
Sometimes, if I'm feeling daring, I cross streams as if I'm in the scene from Ghostbusters.
Sometimes I slam it in reverse as if doing a handbrake turn in a car chase from the French Connection.
That's what I do.

Then I quickly zip up and swim for it.

**THE DRAWING SAYS IT BEST
OR
DO YOU WANT ME TO SAY IT WORSE?**

when I licked
MDMA
off the breasts
of the girl in the pure white suit
who was wearing no underwear
at the after party
of the gay wedding
this is how I felt
(see previous drawing)

A EUROPEAN FOLK TALE ANALYSED, BROKEN UP AND REASSEMBLED IN AN ABSTRACT FORM

Vincent Van Gogh had been running around the fields picking sunflowers, and when he had gathered so many that he could carry no more, he remembered his good friend Pablo Picasso, and set out through the dark forest to see him.

Vincent was surprised to find Picasso's cottage door standing open, and when he went into the room, he had such a strange feeling that he said to himself, "Oh dear! How uneasy I feel today, when at other times I like being with Picasso so much." He called out, "Good morning Picasso," but received no answer. So he went to the bed and drew back the curtains. There lay Picasso with his cap pulled far over his face, and looking very strange.

> "Oh! Picasso," said Vincent, "what big ears you have!"
> "All the better to hear you with, Vincent," was the reply.
> "But, Picasso, what big eyes you have!" he said.
> "All the better to see you with, my dear Vincent."
> "But, Picasso, what large hairy hands you have!"
> "All the better to paint you with."
> "Oh! but, Picasso, what a terrible big mouth you have!"
> "All the better to eat you with!"

Scarcely had Picasso said this, than with a single bound he was out of bed and swallowed up Vincent in one gulp! When Picasso had appeased his appetite, he lay down again on the bed, fell asleep and began to snore very loudly.

Henri Matisse was just passing the cottage, and thought to himself, "How the old man is snoring! I must see if he wants anything." So he went into the room, and when he came to the bed, he saw Picasso lying on it.

"Do I find you here, you old sinner!" said Matisse. "I have long sought you!" But just as he was going to shoot him, it occurred to him that Picasso might have devoured another great artist, and that he might still be saved, so he did not fire, but took a pair of scissors, and began to cut open the stomach of the sleeping Cubist.

When he had made two snips, he saw Vincent's large red nose shining, and then he made two more snips, and the artist sprang out, crying: "Ah, how frightened I have been! How dark and surreal it was inside Picasso's belly. Thank you for saving my life Matisse."

Even though Vincent had lost an ear in the intense struggle, he quickly ran to fetch great stones with which they filled Picasso's belly, and when Picasso awoke, he wanted to run away, but the stones were so heavy that he collapsed at once, and fell dead.

Matisse continued to snip away and created a large paper cutout from Picasso's skin, which he called The Snail.

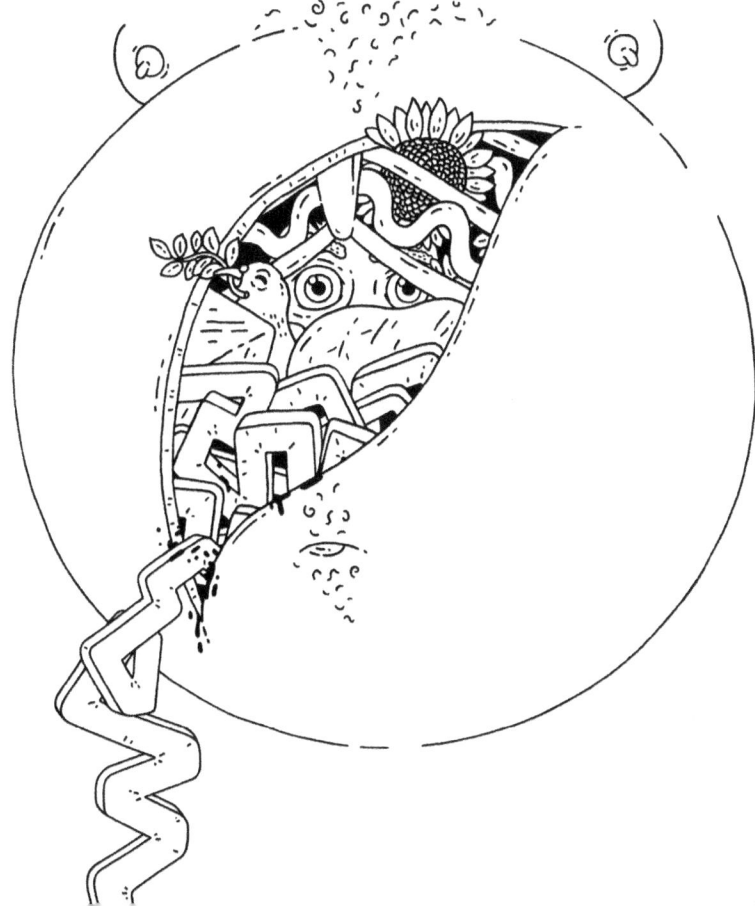

PETER PAN GOGH

He sprung shadowless
Ticking and dreaming
Wormed his way wide-owl-eyed
From the mad-swampy-Pollock-like-womb-gloom

Chrome Yellow Oil and Turpentine hand
Hooked from the Never-Never Land
Clinging tight to the old man's chest
Began to suck energetically on Picasso's swollen breast
An Absinthe and full fat protein pasteurized fest

This world one-big-fucked-up-dot-to-dot art installation gone wrong
The Doctor put him on Milk and Alcohol like in the Feelgood song
Plastering the moon with paint like a lunatic impressionist Neil Armstrong

That's one small step for man
One giant leap for Peter Pan

ManCruelManKindManCrawlManFind
Was it love or the moonshine
That made him go blind?

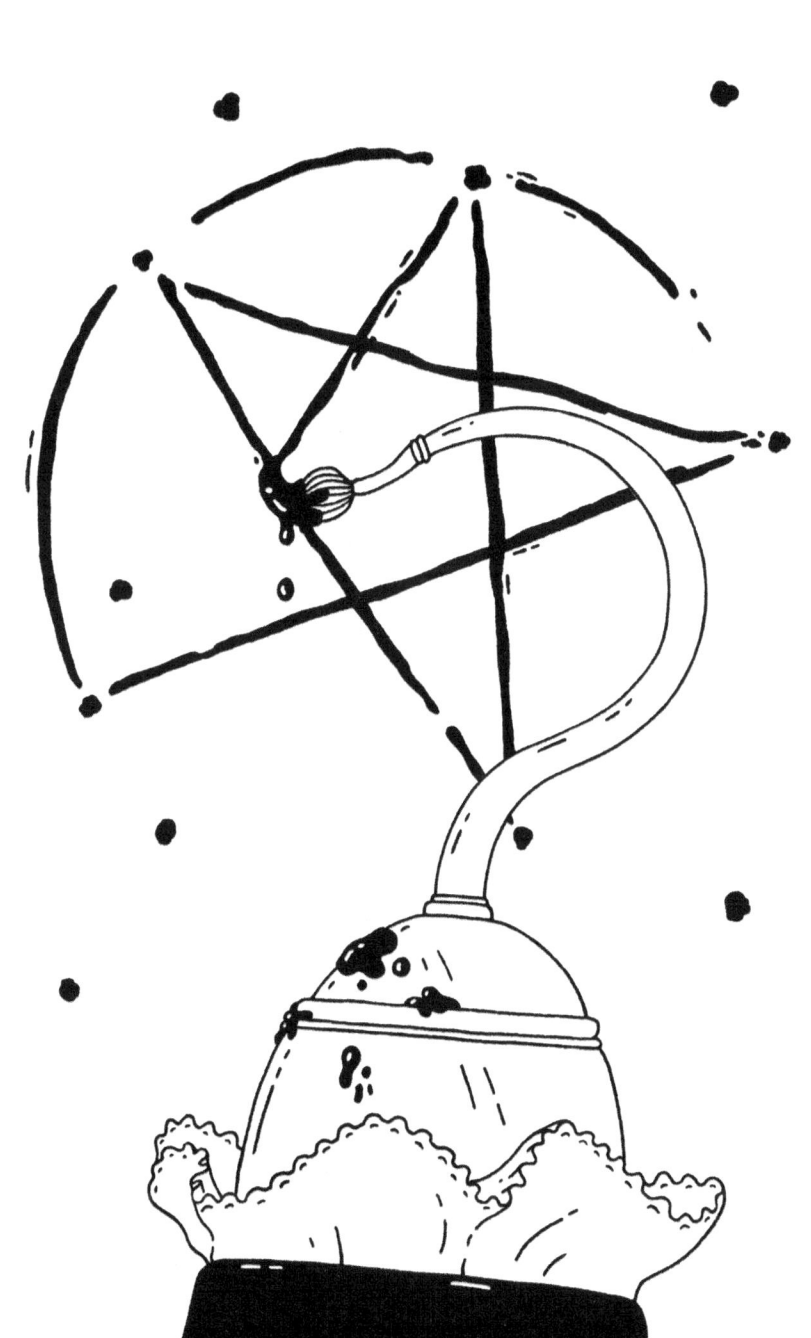

WHAT IF I SAW YOUR SADNESS THROUGH THE SWIRLING HAZE OF OCTOPUS TENTACLES?

What if Captain Hook had been a painter instead of a pirate?
What if John Lennon had been a postman instead of a dreamer?
What if Van Gogh had cut off his arm instead of his ear?
What if you cried when you are happy and laughed when you felt fear?

What if Bowie is a Starman waiting in the sky?
What if clouds were shapeless and the deserts flowed and weren't dry?
What if your friends weren't really friends but all U.F.OEs?
What if when rainwater mixed with engine oil it created nightmares instead of rainbows?

LENNON MADE LOVE TO A LETTERBOX

Imagine there's no postcards
It's easy if you try
No stamps or letters
To send a reply
Imagine all the postboxes
Boarded up and grey

Imagine a family
Trying to cross an ocean on a plastic tea tray
And drowning
Imagine
It's easy

Imagine a thousand people
With no drinking water
Dying of thirst
Imagine
It's easy

Imagine a million people
Watching a crap singing competition on television
Imagine it
It's easy

Imagine there's no compassion or empathy
And no one gives a shit
Imagine it
It's easy

All you need is love
But there's so little to go around these days
All you need is money
There's a lot of money
But you can't have any
Imagine that

Imagine
Imagine having love and money
And an idea how you're going to use it

Imagine hugging a post box
And licking the dog piss off it
Imagine

A pillar of the community
A first class second class working class hero
Privatise the postal system
Leave the public purse with zero
Shut down the local post office
Replaced it with Cafe Nero
A cold cast iron cylindrical cuddle
Is your greatest fearo
Lennon was a poet
Liverpool's Shakespearo
He's getting very intimate
He'll take it up the rearo
We'll write a postal service epitaph
It'll make you shed a tearo

Yo what dy'a know Yoko Ono
Oh no Yoko Ono
You don't know the post office woe

All we are saying
Let's give post a chance

Yoko's gone
Eggman's gone
John's imagination's gone

Once upon a post office lived
Postman John Postman John
Postman John and his cat has gone
It's a con, it's a con, it's a con, it's a con

Imagine there's just junk mail
With no postman to call
No letters left in the hall
Just a virtual inbox in a virtual wall
Delete all

IT'S WHERE THE HEART IS

My brother left home and never came back
He didn't leave a contact number or change of address
I miss him
So I wrote him a love letter and copied it out over a billion times
1.5 billion times to be exact
Blistered my hand and fingers on my Bic pen
Licked 1.5 billion envelopes
Spent a small fortune on stamps
Then I sent it to every household in the entire world
So that he would definitely receive it in the post

**YOUR LOVE IS A SHOWER OF
METEORS HITTING DISTANT MOONS**

Punched a hole in my ripped-out heart
With the font hammer of my Olivetti Lettera typewriter
Kept pounding the heart key like an out-of-tune piano
Over and over
Until it bled the page red

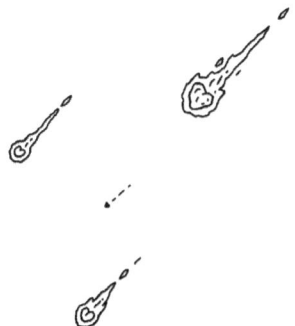

NIGHT BUS

It feels like Armageddon
But it's probably just bedtime

＊ ENJOY THIS BOOK WITH A HOT BEVERAGE.

Lightning Source UK Ltd.
Milton Keynes UK
UKOW05f2131110717
305131UK00002B/474/P